INTRODUCTION

In business, putting on a 'song and dance' can refer to pitching or selling, and negotiations are often referred to as, 'dancing back and forth'. Even though I'm not much of a dancer in the literal sense, I have found in my own entrepreneurial journey that there are many metaphors in dance that can be applied to growing a business and reaching success.

Starting your own venture requires an array of skills and disciplines that ultimately culminate into what we call entrepreneurship. Being an entrepreneur is a sum that is greater than its parts -- more than just being good at multitasking, more than just being good at networking, more than just being good at raising money. Like a dancer who is able to perform; applying years of instruction without putting any awkward, single, discernible lesson on display, a masterful entrepreneur makes success look like it happened overnight.

Here then are your dance lessons in entrepreneurship to help you avoid as many mistakes and missteps as possible, and also find your rhythm to overnight success.

CHAPTER ONE

Timing, Not Time Management

Many aspiring entrepreneurs ask me, "When is the best time to start my business?" I say, better to ask: how much money can you raise from your family and friends, how long can you moonlight until your boss fires you, and how long until the state puts your children in foster care, or your spouse leaves you because you can no longer provide for them! The answer? There is never a perfect time to start a business, or as Mark Twain put it, "There are two times in a man's life when he should not speculate: when he can't afford it and when he can."

Instead, we should ask, what is the best *timing* for starting my own business? The answers elicited from *that* question are much more profound.

If I could distill my entrepreneurial experience into one key lesson, it's this: being a successful entrepreneur is about timing, not time management. Time management is a learned structure used for measurement. Timing is an organic awareness of the patterns and rhythms of everyday life that surround and inform us. For the entrepreneur, listening to the rhythm of the marketplace is paramount.

Often, new entrepreneurs hack at their productivity as

though time were the enemy. As they attempt to transition from employee to employer, or researcher to business leader, the tendency is to think that the same rules for success should apply. They don't. Learned skills directed immediately towards productivity may actually do more harm than good and hobble resilience, flexibility and responsiveness -- all key traits for the entrepreneur. If you are wound up in the details of time management, you may not have your mind open enough to recognise an unexpected opportunity to move forward.

Most experienced dancers say that rhythm is a gift, and that many advanced dancers are 'naturals', but plenty of people can still learn to dance because everyone has some kind of rhythm. Can new business owners tap into their yet undiscovered sense of 'timing' even if they are brand new to entrepreneurship? Yes! Many dancers never thought they could dance because they didn't know how to listen to the music. In business, the ability to hear the notes of opportunity ringing all around you can determine future success. Once you understand how to listen and find the rhythm, then you can dance.

If your life has been a steady march up to this point, then it can be very difficult to make adjustments -- like trying to Cha Cha to a Waltz. You will be out of sync and quickly frustrated. First, know that the early lessons are messy and awkward for everyone. Then, put away the productivity tools, rulers, double-standards and start listening to the rhythm of your marketplace. Your path to success will be uniquely yours, and completely unfamiliar from whatever autobiography you've read or biopic that you've watched on Netflix.

Once an idea inspires you, you will need to start researching the marketplace in which your idea will become a business. New questions will take the place of older ones. Is your business idea new, competitive, too early, or too late? Does your idea provide a solution to someone else's problem? Is your idea a new marketplace unto itself? Either way, the best time to start the business won't depend on trends in the stock market, or your boss letting you moonlight, or the enrollment window for a startup accelerator program. More often than not, once you recognize an opportunity, you will realize that the best time to start your business was *yesterday*.

At the writing of this chapter, the world is still recovering from the COVID-19 pandemic and the various ways it has changed our lives. One unexpected result of the pandemic was the data from the U.S. Census Bureau that reflected a 15% increase in new business formations, up nearly 200,000 from 2019.[1] Is a pandemic a good time to start a business? You might not assume so, but apparently 200k more American entrepreneurs did.

Among them were my business partners at Shield Pals, a personal protective equipment (PPE) brand that attempts to ease anxiety in pediatric healthcare by incorporating fun and friendly characters into the PPE itself, turning an anonymous doctor into a friendly fox, cat, or dog. Husband and wife team, Chris and Tracy McCormick, were forced to shutter Hatch Exhibits, their exhibit production company that they had built into a $6MM/year business, and furlough over 30 employees. Chris saw the Governor of New York on a televised press conference put out the call for PPE and ventilators. As Chris thought about this, he realized he had the equipment for manufacturing face shields and gowns. As part of his outreach to friends with healthcare connections, he contacted me for help getting specifications for face shields and gowns from Johns Hopkins University where I am a Mentor-In-Residence for their technology ventures program. Within 2 weeks, Chris and Tracy had hired back all of their furloughed employees, and then some. Knowing this might be a fleeting business due to the pandemic, we strategized how this company could become a larger brand name with a lasting business model beyond the pandemic. For that to happen, the problems solved would not be supply shortages due to the international shutdowns, as much as the anxiety that PPE and other external factors have caused in children who are suddenly more afraid of their faceless doctors and nurses.

Shield Pals not only stayed in business beyond the initial wave of the pandemic, but went on to generate millions in revenue in its first fiscal year while earning a lot of media attention including; features on the TODAY Show, CNBC, Washington Post and more, and became the official face shield of *SpongeBob SquarePants*® and *Star Trek*®. In this case, necessity was the mother of invention, but an understanding of how the marketplace might change is what kept Shield Pals' founders on their toes, allowing them to navigate through the uncertainty -- to *expect* the uncertainty -- caused by the pandemic, and ultimately to build a successful brand. Oddly enough, this wouldn't be the first time a pandemic would play a role in the timing of a new business for myself.

In 2009-2010, a Swine Flu pandemic ravaged North America, and it occurred to me that its progress could be tracked by listening to social media. In early 2011, that idea launched a company and free disease tracking website called Sickweather, which became a disease forecasting company primarily serving the pharmaceutical industry. I founded the company with my friends James Sajor and Michael Belt. In 2012, I entered us into a pitch competition in Washington D.C. called Distilled Intelligence 2.0 created by the now defunct Fortify Ventures. It was my very first pitch competition. I still had my day job and hadn't raised any outside capital. I used my paid time off (PTO) from work to attend and compete in the hopes that the winnings could be used to quit my job and take the company to the next level. I should also mention my wife was nearly 9 months pregnant with our third child, so my PTO was highly coveted, not to mention the added risk created by me driving over an hour away from her should she suddenly go into labor.

We made the cut into the top 10 companies that day, which meant a second, longer pitch as a finalist; and a Q&A session with the judges. It couldn't have gone better, the audience cheered and the judges grinned. That is, until the very last question of the Q&A -- a judge asked, as if rhetorically, "is this your full time job?" I explained that myself and my co-founders were all working 40 hours a week on Sickweather, but that we still had day jobs to provide for our families. There was a collective groan among the audience and judges. Later, a judge approached me, and said that I could've taken the top prize that day if I had answered that last question differently. I realized at that moment, they had expected all contestants to say that they had already quit their jobs. The judges' paradigm of starting a business was confined to the idea that time management and timing were the same, and that entrepreneurship is a series of checkboxes.

There is a perception among some investors that the presence of other commitments in a startup founder's life makes their respective companies more likely to fail, which creates a paradox for the earliest stages of companies who seek funding: You can't raise money until you've committed 100% to the exclusion of everything else in your life, and yet you can't commit exclusively to your startup until you've generated enough money for it to support you. I believe this is flawed logic that not only results in entrepreneurs becoming adversarial and dishonest with investors, but it outright excludes certain demographics of entrepreneurs who simply don't have savings, generational wealth, or other privileges that would otherwise afford them a spotlight on that stage. Pragmatically, this perception of risk by others does impact the ideal *timing* of stepping out on your own and starting your business, but it's not insurmountable. You may just have to dance to the music in your own head for a while until the right investor comes along. One resource is The Kauffman Foundation, a philanthropic organization dedicated to entrepreneurship, and creators of the *1 Million Cups* program of which I am the lead organizer in Westminster, Maryland. 1 Million Cups is a weekly speaking series for entrepreneurs that is an effort by the Kauffman Foundation to make entrepreneurship "radically inclusive" and to change perceptions of who can become an entrepreneur, which is good news, so check them out if and when you become encumbered by adversity or prejudice, or if you simply need a support group of other like-minded entrepreneurs.

A sense of timing can be a little bit different for each person based on their own circumstances, which can change their perceived emphasis on the rhythms in the marketplace. At the writing of this book; I am a founder and/or partner in three different startup businesses and in negotiations for a fourth, as well as an advisor to three others. I am an executive director and president of two non-profits, a mentor-in-residence for the venture fund of a university, a volunteer for three different working groups, committees, and boards, and a devoted husband and father to five children. I used to feel chagrined to enumerate my responsibilities when I measured myself against the time management ruler of others, because these would all be considered distractions by those measures, but I'm much less apologetic now that I understand how the nature of timing works, and how it empowers me and actually affords me *more* time, not *less* time, to wear so many hats. And no, this has nothing to do with '*work-life balance*'.

WORK-LIFE BALANCE

Dance lessons don't end when you walk out the door after a class. You take that lesson with you wherever you go, and if you are serious, you practice when you are making dinner, doing chores, or playing with your kids. Learning to dance becomes part of the fabric of your life. There are endless blogs, articles and self help books on the topic of work-life balance. The very notion that you can compartmentalize, and somehow balance your work and life as separate entities, is a by-product of our fascination with productivity. I would argue that the idea of work-life balance doesn't exist and that the two cannot be separated. Sure, you can *try,* but at some point you're going to answer a business email while on vacation. I'm not saying you should take your work laptop on your family vacation, or that you shouldn't seek quiet meditation, rest and relaxation, but don't beat yourself up when your livelihood is indistinguishable from your life -- that's why you became an entrepreneur in the first place and stopped working for other people. Ask any farmer how they reconcile work-life balance and they'll probably look at you like you're crazy. Being a farmer is a lifestyle, and so is being an entrepreneur. To tie a bow on this point, allow me to drag in the good name of one of the most respected investors of our time -- a graduate of the Massachusetts Institute of Technology (MIT), co-founder of Techstars and the Foundry Group, and best-selling author of the 'Startup Revolution' series of books -- Brad Feld.

In 2014, I had committed to a Techstars accelerator program in Kansas City, MO, which meant spending the majority of four months away from my family back in Maryland -- by this time my wife and I had three kids. During the Techstars orientation, Brad Feld joined us from Boulder, CO via a video conference, and I asked his advice for achieving work-life balance which was still a new buzz term at that time. He swiftly admonished the idea of a work-life balance and was the first person to open my eyes to this fallacy. It's not that he was callous or dismissive of my family commitments, he had great recommendations for ways to include my family in the startup journey, such as sending regular postcards for each family member, which I did, and my kids treasure those postcards to this day. He reassured me that I shouldn't feel guilt or regret for pursuing an opportunity that was for the betterment of both myself and my family, and one that so few get to experience, but instead focused on how I could include them in the journey.

Likewise, you will face choices that may seemingly put your personal interests and life at odds with your business interests, but instead see how they benefit each other. You need to make sure the benefits of both the ends and the means will outweigh the negatives. This can sometimes be difficult to discern if you aren't honest with yourself about how much you can actually accomplish and still have time at the end of the day to spend with your loved ones. Certainly if you don't have time for them, or if it doesn't otherwise provide a clear benefit to them, then it's not worth pursuing.

Keeping in step with my family was part of my own dance, and I subsequently included them more and more in my business travels after being apart from them for so long during Techstars. A year later, when I attended 500 Startups in Mountain View, California (another world-class accelerator), and had meetings with Apple in Cupertino, my family was there. We all took a road trip to Silicon Valley and lived out of an AirBnB for over a month. Here they are at Apple's headquarters in 2015 for meeting I had with my developer relations manager:

Photo by Graham Dodge. Left to right: Heather [pregnant with Zane], Flint, Luke, Rex and Dulcinea.

The ability to transition from one opportunity to the other, one responsibility to the other, and engage in several at the same time is a learned skill that is the direct result of focusing on the rhythm of timing, and not time management. Earlier in my career I ignored that rhythm in fear of being branded with a 'Scarlet D' for 'Distraction', afterall, some investors relish in telling you distraction is the common enemy of entrepreneurs who lack the discipline to focus and finish what they started like so many bliss-driven New Year's Resolutions. But when you listen to the rhythm, you can find life between the beats, syncopated steps that can actually help you use one experience to inform the other, so on and so forth. For me personally, this attention to rhythm even helps me to remember when to respond to people without reminders (granted not always when *they* expect me to) and to wake up on time without alarms. Your mileage may vary of course, but your sense of timing may eventually become prescient as you discover new patterns and can anticipate the next beat, as though serendipity was your dance partner.

The only way to learn these skills, as with dancing, is simply - start. Take that first step! You may trip and fall on your face, but just get back up and try again. This is exactly why I emphasize the importance of timing over time management. Your path to success as an entrepreneur isn't a straight, metered line. You will need to be adaptable, resilient, flexible and think on your feet. You will need to be more intuitive and less analytical.

But what about the value of planning and goal setting as it relates to time management? Yes, these are important, as is being a master of your own calendar, but those tools won't provide inspiration or help ease rejection, and as Mike Tyson once said, "Everybody has a plan until they get punched in the mouth."

CHAPTER TWO

Dance Partners

Dancing with the wrong partner is a painful experience that can feel like an eternity. Dancing with the right partner, on the other hand, feels effortless, as though you could dance forever. Likewise, choosing your co-founders, investors and other partners for your venture is critical.

Acrimony between co-founders and investors, and not having the right team, are among the top three reasons a startup company will fail, according to CB Insights, a research company that tracks venture capital investments.[2] It's no wonder that so many entrepreneurs choose to go out on their own without co-founders or help from investors, but being a 'solo-preneur' is fraught with its own challenges.

Whether you are moving with the music, or with a person, dancing is all about connection. Dancing solo denies you the experience of being pushed to improve, or to be accountable for your lead, or follow, while developing a new found kindness and patience. 'Solo-preneurship' can create an echo chamber where there is the possibility your hires will tell you only what you want to hear. Going it alone can also be a red flag to investors who already know that eventually you will need help with various facets of the business and will require sweat equity resources to *bootstrap* the business when financial resources are low. Your lack of co-founders could also be seen as an inability to play well with others; so ideally, you will have co-founders in your business who will be honest with you, support you, and challenge you to be the best version of yourself.

In dance, you never say no the first time someone asks you to dance. If the experience is horrible, you don't repeat your mistakes, and you move on without that partner. It's not that the other dancer isn't a nice person, it's that you can't follow, or lead, a truly bad dancer. Most first time entrepreneurs are limited to a small pool of friends and family as first co-founders. Your responsibility isn't so much making sure that each co-founder is a perfect fit, but rather making sure you have mechanisms in place for changing them out should troubles arise. Here are some best practices for setting up those mechanisms:

- <u>Have a Founders Agreement in writing.</u> You can find free templates online, or I recommend using an inexpensive online legal service, like RocketLawyer, to create one. You can certainly retain an attorney, but at this stage it probably isn't worth the cost, and often an attorney, who is versed in being general counsel, won't understand some of the nuances of startup language. If you can afford them, large firms like DLA Piper, Venable and Cooley have attorneys who specialize in startup formation and venture capital deals.

- <u>Don't split the ownership evenly.</u> This may sound greedy, but you aren't starting a band! You are starting a business with elements of control that have far reaching consequences, later on. Anyone who isn't willing to co-sign a bank loan with you, or put up their personal property as collateral, shouldn't have more than 20% ownership in your company. This is because banks and creditors will expect any founder with 20% equity, or more, to secure and approve loans for the business. Investors will also see a founding CEO with less than 51% equity in their business (prior to fundraising and dilution) as a weakness in their ability to lead. Having less ownership over time due to dilution is expected, but don't start from a weak position.

- <u>Include vesting terms.</u> Vesting refers to the time in which a founder's or shareholder's equity is earned. A big mistake is to allow founders, even yourself, to have fully vested equity at the onset of the company. Instead, have a 2-4 year vesting period in which the ownership is earned over time -- usually in monthly increments. This allows you to part ways with co-founders before they've earned all their equity if they aren't pulling their weight. You can add what's called a "cliff" to your vesting terms, wherein they don't earn any equity at all until after a certain amount of time, but I personally think this is excessive for founders who are putting in sweat equity without pay. Speaking of which...

- <u>Don't promise 'sweat equity' at the exclusion of pay to anyone who isn't a co-founder</u>. In most states it isn't legal due to employment laws. Anyone who is working for 'free' needs to be a co-founder and be part of your founder's agreement. What if you already have a founder's agreement, but need to bring on someone new? Then simply amend and restate the agreement with the new founder(s).

- <u>Define control separate from ownership.</u> This is especially important as you get diluted and lose majority ownership over time. One of the best lessons I learned in Techstars was "ownership doesn't equal control." Which is to say, you can define control and decision making for the company as being held with a certain number of founders, or within the Board of Directors. When you put control into the hands of your Board of Directors, you must choose your directors wisely -- don't just have all of your founders on the Board of Directors as this is problematic if you need to let another founder go. Also, never put employees on your board — employees are inherently transactional, especially those in sales, and they will have a conflict of interest regarding decisions about their own compensation versus the company budget. That conflict of interest will impact everything from reinvesting revenue to their expectations of compensation in the event of a merger, or acquisition.

Investors are partners too, and like co-founders they can be a good fit, or not. In the earliest stages, your investors may be friends and family, or angel investors, and later on they may be venture capitalists (VCs). You may just see them all as 'money' either way, but they are each very different with different expectations about how much their money is worth. The following chart illustrates the relative nature of equity ownership expectations by some of the external partners you may come in contact with, but it is not a precise gauge for financial advice:

	Ownership	Capital Investment
Advisors	2%	$0
Friends & Family	5%	$5,000
Accelerators*	6%	$100,000
Angels	10%	$250,000
VCs	20%	$1,000,000
Sharks	50%	$50,000

* Accelerators are usually non-dilutive until equity conversion trigger

Besides differences in stages, there are generally two categories of money: 'smart money' and 'dumb money'. That's to say, there is a sophistication to those who call themselves 'smart money' compared to first time investors trying to redistribute their wealth. It's true that you want to avoid first time investors, but not all self proclaimed 'smart money' investors are actually experienced with the entire life cycle of the startup, and not all 'dumb money' (read: silent) investors are inexperienced. Ideally, you want investors who have both the experience of investing, and the patience not to meddle too much in your day-to-day business, because that meddling, no matter how well intentioned, can kill your business, like Lennie in John Steinbeck's *Of Mice and Men* petting this mouse in his pocket too hard. Speaking of killing pets...

SCHRODINGER'S STARTUP

Schrodinger's Cat is a Quantum Mechanics paradox when a cat is placed in a box with something that can kill it, usually something radioactive. The cat is both alive and dead until the observer opens the box to look inside. It's meant to illustrate how particles can exist in multiple states at the same time. Similarly, early stage startup companies with various risks to solvency (i.e. aren't profitable yet) share this paradox. Startups equally have the potential to become wildly successful, as well as insolvent. Even so-called *unicorns*, startups valued at a billion dollars or more, that have raised hundreds-of-millions of dollars, suffer from this paradox, so long as they aren't profitable. Until either profitability, or insolvency actually occurs, success is often in the eye of the beholder, and by simply opening the box, the observer can trigger its demise.

I was reminded of this phenomenon by a tweet from a young venture partner of a VC fund. In the tweet, the VC mentioned how she enjoyed reading quarterly updates from her portfolio companies, but complained about how few had included hard metrics for key performance indicators (KPIs). While I can sympathize with the VC, I empathize with the founders. I can only assume that those founders hadn't seen meaning in their own metrics yet, and didn't want to be judged on those metrics until they were less subjective. In other words, they weren't ready to open the box. And, for good reason.

Investors have the power to determine the fate of a startup

by starting a chain reaction that can lead the company to a premature liquidation event -- essentially, opening the box too soon. There is a funny bar scene from HBO's 'Silicon Valley' that is a satirical example of this phenomenon when Goolybib's founder has an epiphany that if he had taken less money then he wouldn't have lost control of his company to investors and been forced to sell his company at a loss -- this is followed by a series of expletives. By the way, if you haven't seen 'Silicon Valley', it's a profoundly accurate and insightful glimpse into the tech startup world. Certainly not all startups are so fragile, and not all VCs are so destructive -- and sometimes both are resilient and confident enough to keep what's in the box a surprise for an IPO or exit.

Indeed transparency and cooperation between startups and their investors is not only beneficial, but critical. However, sometimes it seems that startups are sacrificed on the altar of 'fail fast' because of the impatience, or subjective criteria from their investors. It's in these cases that failure can be avoided -- usually just by the founder being better at managing expectations and effectively communicating milestones for both positive and negative outcomes with reasonable contingency plans for the latter -- but for the sake of the dance metaphor let's just say it's by choosing a partner who won't step on your toes.

Just as there are ways to mitigate the impact of a bad co-founder, you can also protect yourself from a bad investor with the proper investment mechanism and terms. If you are raising outside funding from investors there are a few basics you should know about what is negotiated and why:

1) your business formation will dictate whether you can offer options, warrants, equity, future equity, or profit interest units. Generally speaking, in the United States, your choices are C-Corp or Limited Liability Corporation (LLC). A C-Corp can also be a public benefit corporation (B-Corp), and a LLC can also be a S-Corp. Most investors will only invest in a C-Corp or B-Corp since tax liability in the ownership of those businesses flows through

to the corporation (until its shares are liquidated), whereas the tax liability for a LLC or S-Corp flows directly to the owners. Therefore, equity ownership in a C-Corp/B-Corp is much more favorable. For a LLC/S-Corp you would want to be issued what are called profit interest units instead, which is effectively the same as equity ownership, but with different tax implications. LLCs and S-Corps are the most popular form of business in the United States because most small business owners don't raise venture capital. They are preferred because the business owner and business are considered one and the same, and therefore are only taxed once, whereas a C-corp gets its profits taxed AND distributions to its owners taxed. Be sure to discuss these options with your attorney or accountant.

2) the valuation of your company is highly subjective until you have a few years of revenue, so instead you will negotiate based on a reasonable valuation limit known as a *valuation cap*, and often based on a discount percentage of that cap. For example, a 20% discount on a $2MM valuation cap means they will get 20% more equity for their investment whenever the shares convert to equity, effectively as if they invested at a valuation of $1.6MM, if that $2MM cap is reached,

3) ownership is negotiated based on either 'pre-money' or 'post-money' valuation, so be sure to understand which one you are negotiating with your investor. A $2MM investment on $2MM *pre-money* valuation reflects 50% ownership to the investor, whereas a $2MM investment on a $2MM *post-money* valuation reflects 100% ownership to the investor,

4) investors will usually ask for a class of shares known as *preferred* or a *preference,* which means they get paid back their investment before other shareholders (but not before creditors) in the event of a liquidation, and sometimes they try to negotiate a multiple of that preference. For example, a 1x liquidation preference is equal to their initial investment, whereas a 2x liquidation preference means they expect to at least make twice

their investment before others get paid, so on and so forth,

5) and if the terms negotiated are based on a convertible note (instead of an exchange of equity) they will often ask for a repayment term of 1-5 years when they can be paid back in full as if a loan, but if they are not paid back or not converted to equity within that term then they start to earn interest per annum, eg, 2-5% interest each year.

There are many more books on the nuance of investing advice and how to negotiate with investors, so I won't dig much deeper than that. In particular, I can recommend the chapter on fundraising in the book 'Do More Faster' by David Cohen and Brad Feld.

WITH PARTNERS LIKE THESE…

My current obsession is with the various failed businesses and investments of Samuel Clemens that stripped him of his Mark Twain fortunes. We all know of Mark Twain, the humorist, but much less of Samuel Clemens, the investor and entrepreneur who lost his home and most of his wealth. While he certainly made a lot of mistakes, perhaps his biggest mistakes were in his character judgment of various business partners. In a wonderfully written Time Magazine article from 2016 titled 'The 19th-Century Start-Ups That Cost Mark Twain His Fortune', journalist Richard Zacks wrote:

Twain had a personal interest in the business [of publishing]*: he was convinced he had been cheated by publishers for years. Back in the late 1860s, Elisha Bliss of the American Publishing had handed young Twain a rube's meager 5% royalty on Innocents Abroad and sworn to pay him half of net profits on all future books and never did. Twain devoted a circle of hell to former business partners. The writer would later describe Elisha Bliss as "a tall, lean, skinny, yellow, toothless, bald-headed, rat-eyed professional liar and scoundrel… It is my belief that Bliss never did an honest thing in his life, when he had a chance to do a dishonest one."*

The spit and venom of Twain's take down reveals a brutal honesty about the experience of dealing with bad business partners, and I can't help but laugh at the veracity of his hurt and disdain for his former partner. It is impossible not to be affected by such betrayals. Almost everyone has had their share of bad partners, but to publicly describe them as, for example, "a short, rotund, ruddy-complexioned, cheap-hair-dyed, alcoholic, professional liar and Canadian who never did an honest thing in her life, when she had a chance to do a dishonest one," would be contrary to the poise in which a capable entrepreneur must handle this sort of thing. Better to whisk that person up into a Viennese Waltz and dance around the room before you place them in a chair leaving them dizzy and wondering, what just happened? Cut those bad partners loose and do it with style! And remember, your future success will always be the best remedy to the hurt caused by bad partners, so don't bother looking back.

My final point on choosing the right partner is about working with family members. I've often heard it said that you should 'never do business with family,' but I think so long as you follow the same professional framework of choosing a partner that I've outlined in this chapter, then working with family should be fine. Yes, working with family can strain that relationship, but one of the benefits of family is that those relationships tend to be more resilient. The problem is when people take a family relationship for granted and don't think about the professional needs of that family member -- and that starts with setting the same expectations with them as you would any other outside partner or investor. Don't take any business partner for granted, family or otherwise.

CHAPTER THREE

Entrepreneurial Fortitude

Every dance studio has a set of core principles or values that they instill in their dancers to prepare and prime them for competition, such as; respect, determination, creativity, etc. Various startup accelerator programs for entrepreneurs nurture similar values to help their founders develop what I like to call entrepreneurial fortitude. These values and principles aren't just platitudes, they are key emotional pillars to protect you from the inevitable onslaught of competition, cynicism and sabotage. To fight this, you will need to remember the pillars of entrepreneurial fortitude which I've distilled down to a mnemonic 3-H alliteration of: Hope, Hap and Help.

Hope is where entrepreneurial fortitude begins. Hope that your idea will turn into success and the co-founders, business plan, etc, will come together to form that goal. But, hope is often seen as naïveté, or even recklessness -- especially by those steeped in a cowardly corporate culture where innovation and reaching beyond your role is feared, snuffed out and punished; which happens to be the motivation for the antagonist in every movie made about dancing. Don't lose that hope because (to borrow from Dirty Dancing) *nobody puts Baby in the corner!*

The flag of hope is also seen as an arrogant defiance by

those swimming in the thick muck of a conventional system. They will stop at nothing to take it down, so be prepared for a fight. Challenges against your hope will come from everywhere including from your friends, family, co-workers, competitors and even your own investors. But, don't forget that there are good reasons for your hope. Either you have domain expertise, or have identified a clear need in the marketplace for your solution, or you have a product that is already getting positive signals and validation from the marketplace. The longer you can persevere, the more likely you will be able to succeed.

Unfortunately, being a hopeful entrepreneur only gets you so far. There is a large amount of luck -- or *hap* (another word for luck) -- that plays a role in the success of your business. But, luck has its own components: preparation and opportunity. Oprah Winfrey once said, "I believe luck is preparation for meeting opportunity. If you hadn't been prepared when the opportunity came along, you wouldn't have been lucky."

If you are prepared for an opportunity, then you aren't a *hapless* victim of circumstance. Sometimes this requires patience, and one of my favorite scenes about patience is from *Boardwalk Empire*, when NYC kingpin Arnold Rothstein offers his sage advice to Atlantic City kingpin Nucky Thompson, who is getting worked up after bad advice by a gangster named John Torrio:

Torrio: "What are you gonna do?!"

Nucky: "What would you do, John?"

Torrio: "Kill the prick!"

Nucky: "I'm under indictment. The Feds are up my ass."

Torrio: "Then take it with you. Retire somewhere."

Nucky: "Take what? All my money's tied up in a land deal!"

Rothstein: "Nothing."

Nucky: "I beg your pardon?"

Rothstein: "You have no move, Mr. Thompson. You do nothing."

Torrio: "He's under attack, Arnold!"

Rothstein: "All the more reason for patience. I've made my living, Mr. Thompson, in large part as a gambler. Some days I make 20 bets, some days I make none -- weeks, sometimes months in fact, I make no bets at all because there simply is no play. So I wait, plan, marshal my resources, and when I finally see an opportunity, and there is a bet to make, I bet it all."

Torrio might as well be saying: sell the company! ... replace the leadership team! But Rothstein has the *entrepreneurial fortitude* to see past the reactionary options being presented. The situation is no less dire, but Rothstein is actually mitigating the additional risk that would come from Torrio's suggestions, and therefore helping to improve the chances of a better outcome. This can be infuriating to impatient people who don't share your perspective of risk.

The third and final pillar of entrepreneurial fortitude is *help*. When you are being helpful, you earn respect from those you are helping, which builds your network and can pay dividends down the road. Being helpful also has an immediate benefit to yourself as an exercise in understanding and crystallizing *how you know what you know*.

If you are helping others, you are indexing your own experience and evaluating your past decisions -- thereby helping yourself. Furthermore, if you lack the ability to accept or receive help from others, you will be abandoned by those around you. This is another reason why I recommend that solo-preneurs (those entrepreneurs who attempt to startup businesses alone) find co-founders, and that startups get into accelerators. Your ability to receive help is often equal to your ability to help yourself. Take for instance, the Flat Earth Society.

In 2006, I cried with laughter at the posts on a Flat

Earth forum about how penguins were food for ice wall guards. Somewhere buried in the various attempts at reasoning with the Flat Earthers, one of the Spherical Earthers noted how interesting it was to evaluate *how we know what we know* in order to argue and reason against the ridiculous claims and compromised physics of a flat Earth. As a result, he crystalized what he knew to be true about why the Earth is in fact round, citing satellite photography, GPS and gravity to name a few. Unfortunately, his helpfulness fell on deaf ears, but at least he got something out of it by reaffirming what he knows to be true. The same happens for me whenever I am mentoring other entrepreneurs. They may or may not heed my advice, but I get something out of it either way.

Be hopeful, be hapful, and be helpful. If you can identify and focus on these qualities in yourself, you will have the entrepreneurial fortitude needed to venture out and succeed in this world -- whether it's round or flat.

CHAPTER FOUR

Endurance & Discipline

With the aforementioned values in mind, you now need to understand how to enable them. Knowing those values isn't the same as practicing them. For the dancer, if you don't go to the dance studio then you aren't going to be instilled with those values to become a better dancer. For both the entrepreneur and the dancer, the two ways in which you apply those values is through endurance guided by discipline.

Many trailblazing founders will receive emails from investors that contain the dreaded phrase, 'sorry, too early' (read: you'll shoot your eye out, kid!). But, wait a minute, doesn't the early bird get the worm? Nope - not in the world of startups. That specific bird/worm idiom refers to being the first person at the opening of an existing marketplace with pre-existing opportunities; which is not the same as being the first person to have an idea about a new marketplace, or a new opportunity that doesn't yet exist. Think if you were to show up to a Farmers Market that is actually the next day -- were you early, or wrong?

Plenty of startups raise millions of dollars on bloated valuations, but then vanish because they are too early and undisciplined with their spending. Instead of denying the poor timing of your venture, start planning for the long game. It may seem counter-intuitive, but most startups don't think they'll have to worry about playing the long game when raising money. *"My idea is groundbreaking, so I need $2 million ASAP on a $4 million pre-money valuation!"* Do they need that much capital because they are building a groundbreaking technology, or because they are too early for the marketplace and need more time?

My first startup was called NotFilms, a home video publishing website that I co-founded in 2000 with Clayton Graul. It was 5 years ahead of the marketplace in which YouTube succeeded. It was too early. Even the branding was all wrong -- named in response to sites like AtomFilms which streamed videos (sorry *films* *sips wine*) of student filmmakers -- which was also too early. But then again, almost everything in 2000 was too early. Remember DEN.net? Probably not, but they were very well financed and produced original streaming shows 15 years before Netflix. The problem with NotFilms, and many other streaming video sites at that time, was the fact that most people were still on dial-up modems and video was the size of a matchbook. The marketplace simply wasn't ready. When this happens you should stop, take a breath and re-evaluate. You will be well served to slow your roll, and bootstrap until the market catches up to you, or find a product-market fit by some other means. For Netflix, that meant starting as a DVD mail subscription service until more consumers had broadband streaming capabilities.

BOOTSTRAPPING

Bootstrapping is the term used in startup and venture capital nomenclature to refer to anytime when a business forgoes outside fundraising and uses their own existing resources to build their products and services in order to take them to market. It's modern reference comes from usage of the term bootstrap in software development, which in turn likely comes from the idiom "to pull oneself up by one's bootstraps," which originated in the 19th century from this line in the Workingman's Advocate: "It is conjectured that Mr. Murphee will now be enabled to hand himself over the Cumberland river or a barnyard fence by the straps of his boots." [3]

If you don't have co-founders and can't otherwise build a product on your own, then you don't have much hope for bootstrapping in the early days or surviving the 'Valley of Death' between funding rounds. Valley of Death is another term you will hear often, referring to the stage(s) between funding rounds prior to profitability when most early stage startups fail. These are the times when your team needs to keep building and earn their sweat equity. Some people refer to bootstrapping as being mutually exclusive to raising capital, but I don't think so. There are plenty of times when I've had to bootstrap between funding events. This tends to happen when the money raised previously isn't quite enough to get to the next milestone. Your startup learns a lot during these times, and often exercises better decision-making skills under pressure... like when you also need to pee real bad (as evidenced from a study showing that people make better choices when they have a full bladder).[4]

Bootstrapping also means you should spend equal amounts of time on developing leads and a sales pipeline, as you would do on fundraising. You'll need that revenue when investors are unconvinced, and of course to also create a return on investment (ROI) for yourself and your investors. The prime directive of a startup CEO is to make sure the company doesn't run out of money, but that doesn't mean it all needs to be from the same source. It's ok if it takes some fundraising to get to product-market fit when your product is actually marketable and generates some revenue, but don't ever confuse funds from investors as income, or revenue. Too many startups celebrate their fundraising rounds as though it validates their business model, but it doesn't. In a word, *hustle!* Get your business to profitability, or at least break-even, as soon as possible. And don't be ashamed, or intimidated if you need to take out a loan, apply for a grant, or raise capital to get there. That's what those funds are for.

COMPETITION

Leaders get arrows in the back AND the front, so don't worry if some of your competitors get out in front of you during this time... let them take an arrow or two, and learn from their successes and mistakes. The best dancer is always sought after and not always in an honorable way. Many times another dancer might rudely inject themselves with a better dancer to make themselves look good, or try to steal another dancer's choreography entirely. It's the same for innovative leaders and their businesses, they are the ones everybody wants a piece of; for good, or for bad. I know how frustrating it is to watch copycats get millions in funding using strategies that you created, but don't let it discourage you. Your investors may panic (the good ones won't), but you should remain calm and put one foot in front of the other. Not only is imitation the best form of flattery, but more importantly, competitors are validation and a good sign that the marketplace is catching up to you. Just don't let them get too far ahead. MySpace comes to mind.

The operator of an Esports and tabletop gaming lounge came to me once with his voice cracking from the stress of a new competitor emerging in his market area. He was distressed that this new competitor was benefiting from the lessons learned by his business and the playbook that he and his partners had worked so hard to establish. I reminded him that competition in this case also contributed to the density of these activities in the region, which would serve to benefit both businesses by creating more gravitational pull for their mutual customers (in this case, gamers). More succinctly, I compared this phenomenon to the early days of baseball franchises and used the New York Yankees and New York Mets as a metaphor for how these businesses could co-exist, and to imagine his business as the superior Yankees franchise, and the competitor as the inferior Mets (apologies to any Mets fans). Despite being an Orioles fan, this metaphor helped allay his worry and stress by putting this new competitor into the perspective of a thriving marketplace with an increasing demand for their mutual services.

REJECTION

In the negotiation handbook, "Never Split The Difference" by Chris Voss, the former hostage negotiator explains that, "no is the first step toward yes." I've also found this to be true. If an investor or a business prospect says 'no'; well, that's great! Not having an answer at all is much worse, and an easy 'yes' can sometimes lead to more frustration. But 'no' usually means that there's something specific they don't like that you could potentially overcome, with time... like being too early. Keep your prospects updated quarterly -- that should include both investors and clients. As you continue to build and respond to feedback, you'll likely overcome all previous objections, and they'll be very grateful you stayed in touch.

People handle rejection differently, and it seems to be determined by their personality types. Whether you subscribe to Myers-Briggs or DiSC for categorizing personalities, there are common personality types that withstand rejection, or easily succumb to it. Those whose personalities are better suited for confrontation can also handle rejection the best because they already are conditioned to letting criticism slide off their backs. Those who are more sensitive or who are more gregarious have a much harder time with rejection because they take it so personally, since they want everyone to like them. For the latter personality types, they can learn to adjust by understanding how to deal with those opposite personality types. Knowing that your prospect is, say, confrontational and analytical, can help you understand not only how to approach them, but how to disassociate personal feelings from rejection.

And remember, rejection is just part of the negotiation process, which as stated in the Introduction of this book, is like dancing back and forth. In Salsa dancing, your dance moves must compliment those of your dance partner. When they advance, you step back, then return with your own advance, so on and so forth, like a parry of the feet. What you don't do is argue with your partner by moving toward them at the same time as they move toward you - that will just result in hurt toes and embarrassment.

ACCELERATION

My co-founders from Sickweather and I eschewed accelerators for the first few years while we were still working our day jobs. This was mostly because we didn't see the need for them as seasoned business owners from a time when accelerators didn't exist (pre-2000s). Back in those early dot-com days, companies themselves played the role of incubators and accelerators as teams would form internally and spin out their own little baby companies. My first company NotFilms was incubated this way within a development company called Black Sheep New Media, and more famously MySpace was spun out of a company called eUniverse. In fact, the entire success of Silicon Valley is built upon this phenomenon. Between 1955-1971, a single company called Fairchild Semiconductor gave birth to over 30 different businesses, affectionately known as Fairchildren, which included such powerhouses as Intel and AMD. Innovative companies are breeding grounds for innovation, whether they are unwitting participants in this propagation, or not.

Accelerator programs recreate this phenomenon and have become launch pads for success, not just for connecting startups to investors, but to one another for continued support well past 'Demo Day' -- the accelerator equivalent of a debutante ball. But finding a good accelerator can be very hard, and even harder to get into. I've had the privilege of attending three of the top five accelerators: 500 Startups, Techstars and Plug and Play Tech Center, and they were all slightly different. Techstars was more hands-on with a smaller cohort and better for early stage companies. 500 Startups provided more autonomy with larger cohorts focused on the growth stage. And, Plug and Play Tech Center was focused on matchmaking between startups and corporate ventures or strategic partners. The greatest value in all of these programs is in the networks themselves. But you get out of it what you put into it, so if you don't work the network, then the network won't work for you. To find accelerators near you, you can search f6s.com, which has a comprehensive list of accelerators, incubators and other programs.

There is also a program created by the National Science Foundation called Innovation Corps (I-Corps) which is operated by various organizations as hubs throughout the United States. I am a mentor for the I-Corps hub at Johns Hopkins University, and I highly recommend it. An I-Corps hub program is a condensed version of what you would learn in all of the aforementioned accelerators, within the span of approximately 4 weeks. Some of these programs, such as the one at Hopkins, offer some non-dilutive grant funding at the end of the program, but these quick programs are mainly for the educational value, and not for the investment that may otherwise come from a traditional accelerator program. There is a longer, 6-month National I-Corps program that resembles more of the traditional accelerator model and that provides funding. Most of the hubs will recommend alumni for the National program as a next level, but companies can also apply to the National program directly, although be prepared to deal with a tedious Federal grant application process.

OUTLAST

If you follow the general guidelines to develop your endurance marked by discipline, you should be able to outlast any disaster and become what some investors call a "cockroach startup." Paul Palmieri, the founder of Millennial Media would characterize this as "grit" -- which is why he calls his venture capital fund Grit Capital Partners. He further defines grit as team endurance -- "Team endurance is when a company or business as a whole comes together to pursue goals, toughs it out through rough patches, and comes up with new and innovative ideas and strategies to navigate along the way."

This applies whether you are an early stage startup or a company in a growth stage. I'm sure companies can develop team endurance at any stage, but when it's baked in from the beginning, then your innovative and groundbreaking ideas will defy the condemning law and logic of being "too early."

CHAPTER FIVE

First Position - Personal Brand

For most kinds of dancing, the beginner must learn where the feet go. The feet are the foundation for the position, balance and execution. Without the feet, the dancer will not get very far. In ballet, dancers learn 5 basic foot positions that are the basis for all of their dance moves. Likewise for the entrepreneur, there are five basic positions for the development of your business: Personal Brand, Company Brand, Pitch Deck, MVP, and Rest.

When I mention **Personal Brand**, I don't mean it in the same sense as an Instagram celebrity, or a 'YouTuber', where your brand and image are one and the same. Rather, this is about establishing yourself as a Subject Matter Expert (SME) in any sphere you want to target, such as: the marketplace, the problem, the solution or the acquisition landscape. Here are some examples:

You've worked in this **marketplace** and understand it through and through, which means you likely understand the problems and potential solutions, but it can also mean you simply understand the dynamics at play and how to leverage them in your favor. Most *Software As A Service (SaaS)* founders fit this description, since they understand the SaaS marketplace first and foremost, regardless of the problem or solution.

You may be an outsider looking in, but have personally or professionally been impacted by the **problem**. When I started Sickweather it was in part because I had been sick with a stomach bug and just wanted to know if something was going around or if there were any reports of food poisoning in the news. I was surprised to learn there was no such thing as real-time disease surveillance in the age of social media. So as a father of little germ factories, I was an expert on the problem.

You've created a **solution** that you suspect will impact similar problems in other marketplaces. You may be an inventor, innovator, developer, scientist, engineer, or manufacturer who can quickly prototype solutions based on your expertise in designing and building. James Dyson famously sells himself as this type of SME in the early commercials for Dyson vacuums.

Maybe you've **exited** a business in the past, or have worked in M&A (mergers and acquisitions) and are now focusing your knowledge on a new marketplace, problem or solution that you know can have a similar outcome. You may be less interested in developing a company as much as flipping a business and providing a quick or sizable return for your investors. You understand opportunities from the perspective of their exit potential across a variety of industries.

If you are a SME in *all* four categories, then the odds for success are in your favor. If not, then you will need to build your team accordingly and fill in the gaps. But, if you are not a SME in *any* of these categories, the odds are against you. Essentially, investors, partners and clients alike need to know why you and your team are the right person/people for the job, and you are the only one who can inform them of this. Your personal brand is all about creating that trust, validation and recognition early on with others whose business you are trying to earn. You can also achieve that by highlighting companies, universities, and certifications that are relevant to your startup, and downplaying or removing any past experience that doesn't mesh with that.

During one M&A negotiation with a strategic buyer, a representative of the buyer explained to me that if I wanted to stay with the company post-acquisition, I would need to focus my LinkedIn profile on the healthcare industry, despite my previous experience in everything from accounting to television production. He didn't want there to be any questions about my expertise in healthcare and so overnight I went from *Graham Dodge - Prop Master on MTV's Wild'n Out, Marketing Director at KatzAbosch, Art Director on GEICO's Caveman's Crib, Creative Director at Fandango Productions*, the list goes on; to simply *Graham Dodge - Healthcare Expert.* It's ok if your personal brand changes, or evolves over time. Just be sure to *own* whichever persona you are promoting. In other words, keep your feet firmly in place! Now is not the time to be humble, self effacing or passive-aggressive. If I had a nickel for every time I witnessed a new entrepreneur apologize for their lack of experience I would probably have enough to fill a sock and hit them over the head with it! Remember these four words whether you are pitching to your best friend, a perfect stranger, or an investor: YOU ARE THE EXPERT. No one else knows your own venture better than you, therefore don't add any apologetics to your introduction or pitch. That doesn't mean you should throw around hyperbole like some Trumpian character, and it doesn't mean you shouldn't admit when you don't know something.

One of the great ironies of being an entrepreneur is the anxiety of being found out as a fraud, or imposter. This is actually referred to clinically as Imposter Syndrome, and every entrepreneur experiences it at some point, but that doesn't mean you should cower to it. Just like any other nervous disorder, or stage fright, it needs to be controlled. Easier said than done, since there are actual frauds and imposters out there who give entrepreneurs a bad name. I have no data to back this up, but I suspect that after Elizabeth Holmes, the infamous founder of Theranos, was exposed in the 2015 Wall Street Journal article entitled, "Hot Startup Theranos Has Struggled With Its Blood-Test Technology" by John Carreyrou, worries of imposter syndrome among would-be entrepreneurs skyrocketed, and may have even prevented some from pursuing their dreams after seeing Holmes' burned in documentary effigy from one film after another throughout 2019-2022. Around the same time, the founders of the infamous *Fyre Festival* were also the subject of numerous negative documentaries. The late twenty-teens were not a good time to be a self-proclaimed entrepreneur. But these bad apples didn't come out of nowhere, they were encouraged and formed by the culture of, "fake it till you make it!"

At some point in time as an entrepreneur you will be expected to "fake it", but don't forget that you are also expected to "make it." The problem with Holmes and others like her is that they were far too comfortable with the "fake it" part of that mantra. And they usually had some co-conspirators in the form of business partners or investors who encouraged that behavior to keep inflating the valuation of their respective companies in the absence of market traction and revenue. That kind of misdirected encouragement can make anyone into an actual fraud. And watching other entrepreneurs commit fraud can make you see that behavior in yourself. To paraphrase Friedrich Nietzche, "if you gaze long enough into an abyss, the abyss will gaze back into you."

It doesn't help matters that founders are expected to push the envelope, to sell the biggest and boldest vision of their company -- to be Steve Jobs, Ray Kroc, Thomas Edison or Elon Musk. Elizabeth Holmes herself tried to emulate the qualities of those visionaries, going so far as to wear a black turtleneck as her personal brand like Steve Jobs, but she lacked actual expertise in all of the aforementioned SME categories: she didn't really understand the marketplace, problem, solution or exit strategy, she only understood the *vision*. But without some expertise, selling a vision is just selling science fiction.

Figure out why you are the right person for your venture, and own it. This is your first position. Without that, nothing else will work.

CHAPTER SIX

Second Position - Company Brand

When a local entrepreneur wanted to open a bookstore on Main Street in Westminster, MD, she was referred to me for some advice, and one of my first questions was about branding. The conversation went something like this:

Me: What do you want to call it?

Them: Bookish.

Me: Cool name… [*clickity clack clack*] … no good domain is available for that… [*clickity clack clack*] … and Simon & Schuster already owns the trademark for that name.

Them: But we like that name. What if we call it Bookish Westminster?

Me: Well, if you ever plan to sell your books online then you would still be infringing on their trademark. And big corporations like Simon & Schuster have legal teams looking out for that sort of thing.

That type of exchange is fairly typical with a first time entrepreneur. Fortunately, in this case they went on to pick another name that was free and clear of trademark infringement and had a top level domain (TLD) availability, e.g. dot-com, a rarity these days. The business is now called Rudolph Girls and their coordinated social media and branding campaigns ahead of their business launch happened to be a terrific lesson in what-to-do right when launching a new business. They sold branded t-shirts to help raise funds, kept followers on social media anxious with anticipation for their opening, offered discounts to those wearing their t-shirts when in the store, shared their personal stories of why they started the business in any media or speaking opportunity they could get, and had both a soft launch and a grand opening that built excitement with followers and local media to the point of lines wrapping outside their doors at both events. For a bookstore launching in a small town in 2021, this was no small feat. And there are two other lessons to be learned here. Do your research before settling on a brand name to make sure that it's actually available, and don't limit your business potential with a brand name that assumes a passive or defensive position in the marketplace. In other words, don't choose a name that would keep you on the run or in hiding from a larger corporation, potentially creating legal problems for yourself later. Startup businesses are tenuous enough without legal woes built into the DNA of the company. Imagine if Rudolph Girls had launched with the name Bookish Westminster -- all of the hard work and flawless execution would have been completely undone by the first *cease and desist* letter for trademark infringement.

I don't know for certain if Simon & Schuster would have ever taken legal action against a small town business like a family-owned bookstore, which would essentially be undermining one of their own distribution channels, but lawyers will be quick to point out that they don't want your infringement possibly causing "confusion" among their client's customers, since trademarks are meant to protect the consumer from that confusion, and not protect the company as a defensive technique or used against would-be competitors (although trademarks are often abused for those purposes). I'll share a funny anecdote about trademark infringement that happened to me, that I also shared with the bookstore owners at that time.

In 2008, I was a partner in an organic skincare business called Kaylala. It was a family-owned business with my wife and her sister as my partners. I was in charge of graphic design, ecommerce, and packaging, while they did all the rest. One of our more novel products was a small tin of hand lotion bon-bons called Hand Candy. You placed the "candy" in your hand, crushed it with your thumb, and rubbed the lotion goodness into your dry hands. Hand Candy came in a few different "flavors", one of which being *White Chocolate Raspberry Truffle*. It became one of our products that garnered some attention from health and beauty bloggers at that time - one of our promo videos for Hand Candy is still trapped in time on Vimeo if you want to track it down. Then, one day, I received a letter from a law firm representing The Cheesecake Factory. It was a cease and desist letter threatening legal action against Kaylala LLC for infringing on their trademark for *White Chocolate Raspberry Truffle*, the flavor of one of their cheesecakes. Luckily, it was a hilarious misunderstanding that didn't go any further when their crack legal team realized that we weren't selling a food product! But a valuable lesson was learned -- *research trademarks for your brands!* Because corporations will find you and shut you down if you infringe on their marks, no matter how small a business you are, or no matter how easily distinguished your brand is from their trademark.

You can't build a company without your brand being defensible, let alone available. And be sure you like it, because your company brand and your personal brand will become synonymous with each other. To this day, many people still refer to me as "Mr. Sickweather." Speaking of which, the branding for Sickweather was chosen because it was a) available across all top-level domains, b) not owned by anyone as a trademark, and c) affordable. I also liked it because it made people think and, more importantly, it made them ask me about it - why did you choose *that* name? Which is helpful when trying to get earned-media attention from reporters and to get news anchors to have fun saying your name on the air. It was a scrappy, guerilla marketing branding choice for a startup with no resources. It was one of the few negative or antagonistic sounding branding choices that I think ended up working well, similar to brands like Rotten Tomatoes, Urban Decay, Pandora, Virgin, Gap, and Hotwire. Some of these interpretations are more subjective than others, but if you think about it, even Apple with its logo design showing Eve's bite mark that cast humanity out of the Garden of Eden was a provocative choice at the time. These kinds of branding choices tend to be embraced by younger customers, and if successful, become as ubiquitous and benign as those brands without any negative connotations.

CHAPTER SEVEN

Third Position - Pitch

Whether it's the 15 second elevator pitch to anyone who will listen, or a 10 page pitch deck to investors, you need to be able to convey the value proposition of your business confidently and concisely. The goal of your pitch should be to elicit responses such as; "oh wow, how did you think of that?", or "how does that work?" Or, ideally, "how do I invest?", "where can I buy it?", etc.

Developing your pitch deck is an important exercise in understanding your business. Notice, I did not say business *plan*. Business plans aren't really used anymore, and thank goodness for that! If you think pitch decks are difficult to write, a business plan takes the pitch deck to a level of tedium that only fans of Tolkien's "other books" can appreciate. Business plans can easily exceed a hundred pages, whereas a pitch deck is approximately ten pages, give or take, and should include the following:

Title Page: Your company branding, tagline and contact info.

Problem: What problem are you trying to solve? Distill it to the main problem, or biggest problem. Don't enumerate problems.

Solution: Your elevator pitch goes here.

How It Works: Explain your solution in slightly more detail.

Marketplace: What market, or industry, does your solution serve, and how big is it? You can usually find some high level analysis by just Googling the industry. If you know the Compound Annual Growth Rate (CAGR), even better! For example, "our marketplace is X, which is worth $12B and has a 10% CAGR." Use the biggest numbers you can find.

Revenue Model: How is the solution going to make your investors rich?

Financial Projections: How rich will they be in 3-5 years? This is usually represented by the "hockey stick graph" (up and to the right) that is defensible by some basic logic. For example, if you have a sales force driven revenue model then your projections could be based on an increase of sales personnel over time. If it's referral driven then you would have a formula for that growth based on network effect. Most investors realize you don't have a crystal ball and they will take this slide with a grain of salt, but they will still expect it to be grounded by reasonable expectations. Here is an example of a 5 year financial projection that also takes into account added dimensions of expenses and net profit vs revenue:

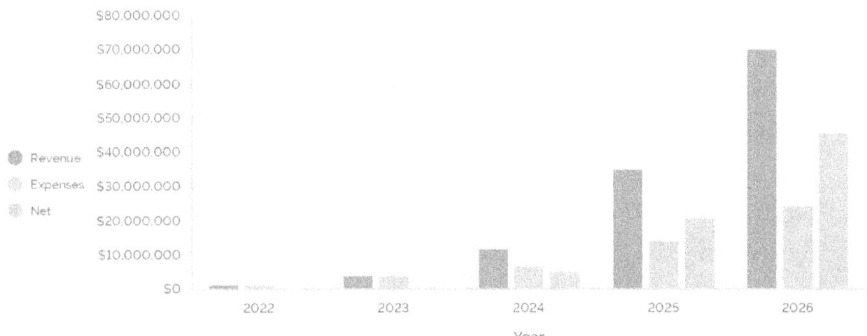

Competition: You can be creative with how you portray your competitors. Steve Jobs usually gave a relative comparison to show how much better his solutions were than those of his competitors, eg if on a graphic of 1-10, 10 being best, his product would be 10 and his competitor would be maybe 3 at best. One of my personal favorite versions of this is to show a double axis quad chart that plots the company and its competitors across a value-based landscape. In this example, my former startup called Garnish is comparing itself to a variety of healthcare funding solutions based on cost and Medical Loss Ratio (MLR):

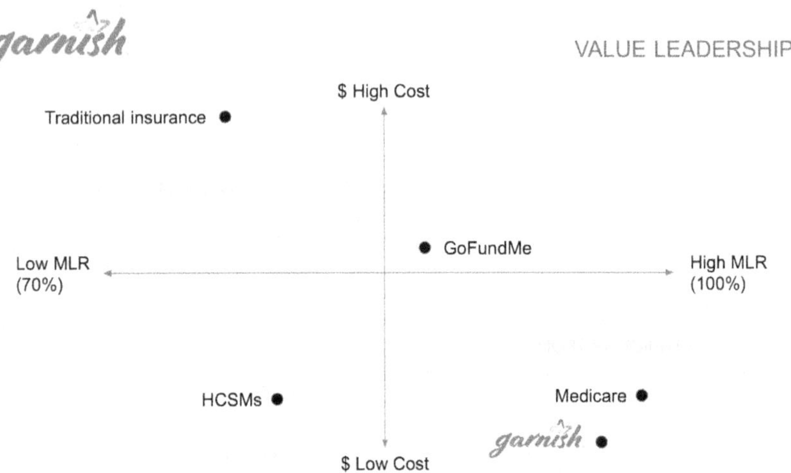

Team: Who are you, and why are you and your team the right team to solve this problem and build this company? This is where you would mention your credentials and/or academic affiliations.

Traction: Don't hesitate to mention any customers, earned media attention, or partners, you may have. Some investors will see anything other than recurring revenue as 'vanity metrics' but that's ok. So long as you aren't drinking your own Kool-Aid it's fine to brag about early successes.

Ask: What do you want or need from the person viewing this deck? If it's money, let them know how much you are raising and if any other notable investors are already 'in'.

There are many variations of the 10 slide pitch deck,

largely popularized by Apple Fellow, Guy Kawasaki, but that's the best order, in my experience. Other popular variations are the "Subject Matter Expert" version which starts with the Team slide and builds from there, or the "Traction Sandwich" that starts and ends with 2 different Traction slides, eg Traction Slide #1 could represent traction with early customers, and Traction Slide #2 at the end could show earned media attention.

Building your pitch deck will help you better understand your business and find any gaps in your plan. Once you create a pitch deck and memorize it, you don't always need to use it. Seems counterproductive, but the best presentations are those when you have a dialog and/or a demonstration. No need to shoehorn a pitch deck into the conversation if it isn't needed. Less is always more when it comes to pitching. Technical founders and engineers tend to have the most difficulty with keeping their pitches lean since they want to explain every detail of their technology or invention. For these founders, they need to realize that investors and customers usually don't care as much about the technology as much as they care about the value proposition. How will your product or service address pain or gain for their customers? Meaning, how will it alleviate a pain point preventing them from being more successful or efficient, or provide them means for gaining more business for themselves?

Your pitch largely is built upon, and served by, the confidence of your personal brand and company brand. When pitching, you need to speak with authority and not flounder on the value proposition. Like a good attorney, you need to anticipate every question and have an answer at the ready. This can be practiced with a friend or family member where you encourage them to pick apart your pitch and keep asking 'why' until the questions fall into a loop or become rhetorical. If presenting in front of an audience, be sure to know your audience and tailor your pitch accordingly.

When I was practicing my pitch for my Techstars Demo

Day in Kansas City, I was approached by producers of the television show Shark Tank to pitch on their show around the same time. This meant memorizing two different pitches that were just similar enough to be maddening and easily confused. However, it was critical that I didn't crossover one or the other to the wrong audience. My pitch for Techstars included slides that tracked with my presentation, whereas my pitch on Shark Tank did not. For Techstars, I was pitching to a largely supportive audience of investors, early adopters, evangelists, and fellow entrepreneurs; for Shark Tank it was also investors, but with a very narrow investment thesis, and then a television audience that needed to be, first and foremost, entertained. I never ended up on Shark Tank, despite being flown out to pitch to its executive producers on the Sony studio lot, with all expenses paid, but it wasn't for not nailing the rehearsed pitch that they coached me through. I can't tell you why I didn't end up on Shark Tank, since I signed an non-disclosure agreement that literally covers the entire universe and for all time, but I can say that *true to their forewarning*, an entrepreneur on Shark Tank can get cut at any point in the process between the very first interview, all the way to post production after taping. But the lesson here is that you need to memorize your pitch well enough to offer any variation based on the audience; forwards, backwards, upside down, or whatever the situation requires.

CHAPTER EIGHT

Fourth Position - MVP

"If you're not embarrassed by the first version of your product, you've launched too late." - Reid Hoffman, Co-founder of LinkedIn

The Minimum Viable Product (MVP) is critical for both raising money and generating customers. Some people confuse a prototype with an MVP, but the operative word is "viable". Even if it's not attractive, can it be used for its intended purpose by real customers? If so, then it's an MVP and not just a prototype.

Your MVP (or MVS if offering a service) will be the result of the Design Thinking Process. The term 'design thinking' originates from the 1950's in reference to engineering and has become widely adopted by universities and corporations for teaching innovation. This is the process by which you recognize a problem, create a solution that you test, get feedback and then repeat, as necessary. The version of the design thinking process that I've found to be the most comprehensive is broken down into 6 parts within 3 main subjects, as follows. (credit to Nielsen

Norman Group, a UX research consulting firm, for this basic outline):

    I.   UNDERSTAND

        A. Empathize: Who are your customers and what makes them tick?

        B. Define: What are the specific pain points that they are experiencing, or specific opportunities that you can create for them?

    II.   EXPLORE

        A. Ideate: What are the potential solutions to their problems?

        B. Prototype: Create a functional version of your solution.

    III.   MATERIALIZE

        A. Test: Test your solution/ prototype.

        B. Implement: Demonstrate your prototype to get feedback.

If you can't build your MVP alone, then you will need to find a co-founder or developer who can. Easier said than done, and that's why most founders don't learn this *fourth position* of the Entrepreneur's Dance. It's also the most expensive position to learn if you are hiring other people to build it.

You might be able to partner with a pre-seed venture studio to build your MVP, but just make sure you define the scope of work clearly. Otherwise, you will give up more equity than you might expect. And beware of the app development companies offering part cash, party equity for their services. Most of them are just inflating their costs by 100%, then discounting by 50%, and will take the other 50% of payment as equity in your company relative to your valuation. It's a shell game where you still paid full price AND gave them equity in your business.

Unfortunately, you will be limited by your resources, and there's no way around getting an MVP before raising capital since investors rarely invest in ideas alone. On rare occasions, an entrepreneur can raise funds on an idea alone, but that's usually because they have already launched or exited another successful business, and investors already trust them, or a market is so hot that investors feel less risk averse. Otherwise, investors want to see real progress or traction. In short, you can't raise money on vaporware, but you also don't want to wait too long to go to market. Understand what is viable, build it, and take it to market.

CHAPTER NINE

Fifth Position - Rest

Everyone knows that a dancer's career is short because their body will eventually give out which is why dancers take great care of themselves, at least the professionals who last the longest, do. Although the entrepreneur might not be drilling on pirouettes or back steps, they also need to take care of their bodies and most importantly, their minds, with diet and exercise. This is when time management skills will serve you well. Make sure you have time for yourself and your own health. There are many anecdotes about entrepreneurial savants who never sleep, or who hike mountains and return with business plans, or who only eat yak butter, pills and fruit, but you will certainly be different and will need to find what works for you.

The body knows when there is something wrong, and will tell you; whether it's by sleeplessness, excessive sweating, constipation, asthma, dry skin, vertigo, crying for no reason, the list goes on. Be intentional and carve out time for self care and rest. Your health, your family shouldn't come second to your venture. In other words, dancers always make sure to take care of their feet.

Resting also gives you time to regain much needed perspective so that when in a tense situation you will be less likely to talk yourself into a corner. I've never regretted not saying more to someone as much as I have regretted having said too much. There is much wisdom in the 'sleep on it' method of decision making.

If you think that 'rest' is not really a business lesson or position, then think of the resting position as a function of your personal brand that can also facilitate networking. This is why golf is so popular among executives - they can network and make deals while doing something they enjoy that helps them clear their head. Same with hiking, fishing, sailing, and any outdoor activity that gets you exercise. And for some people, resting means leaning back with an ice-cold beer, or leaning in with a pumpkin spiced latte. To each their own. The resting position is a way to pace yourself and protect yourself, so that you can endure for longer and be more successful.

This advice may be the most easily said than done of all the lessons in this book. As I write it, I think - I should actually follow my own advice! That's not meant to be humblebrag as though I am some sort of exceptional, productivity workhorse. Instead, I look in the mirror and see someone who has aged much faster than my peers due to stress and overwork, and not for any discernible benefit or reward. To really contemplate this lesson, one must think of their health as their greatest asset, and the lack thereof as their greatest liability. Too often people think of their rest as a currency that can be redeemed for success, or some other brass ring. I'm reminded of a billboard advertising a gym that I used to drive past in Los Angeles during the late 90's that said, "You can rest when you're dead." That seemingly benign marketing ploy was probably responsible for inadvertently misguiding thousands of people to their doom who took it too seriously, myself included, because if you don't rest, then that's exactly what's going to happen to you.

Resting is not the opposite of hustling, or sprinting, or whatever fast-paced descriptor you can think of, it's in fact a necessary part of all of those things. Rest yourself in the same way a dancer rests their own feet because without those, there is no dancing.

CHAPTER TEN

Decisions and Negotiations

D ance is full of making choices and decisions. Every move needs to be carefully considered as it sets you up for the next move. This eventually becomes innate, but at first trying to learn several intricate moves at once can be extremely intimidating. Therefore you need to learn each move in stages. The trick is to break it down. For entrepreneurs, making decisions and negotiating can be paralyzing, but there are steps to ensure you don't stumble.

DECISION-MAKING

When Amazon CEO, Jeff Bezos said in an interview that he only expects "to make three good decisions a day." He was criticized by many shareholders for his laissez faire attitude towards his leadership role in one of the largest companies in the world. But, his approach to decision making should be admired since he was basically saying he didn't have all the answers. Certainly, there are more than three decisions that need to be made at Amazon each day, but only the most important ones, or the ones that only he can answer, should demand his attention.

On a smaller scale, you will likely have the bandwidth to make more than three decisions a day, but that doesn't mean that you can't seek out help. Your ability to parse and delegate decision-making will be a key part of your success as an entrepreneur, and the mechanisms for decision-making that you build early on will help reinforce trust in you by your investors and team alike. Here are some examples of who can help:

Mentors: These are your acquaintances who have domain expertise in areas of business that you don't yet have. This could be another entrepreneur or CEO, or an investor. These are usually unpaid counselors that you can confide in over coffee, or with a phone call. A paid mentor is more likely a coach or consultant. Acknowledging your notable mentors in your pitch deck is a good way to build trust with investors, but since they usually don't have an equity stake in your company, they aren't necessarily considered an asset to the business itself, unlike an advisor, director or officer. However, they could be the types of people you will eventually ask to join your advisory board or board of directors.

Advisory Board: I personally love building advisory boards. They not only associate expertise and trust with your business, but they can considerably extend your network of influence as advocates and cheerleaders for your organization. Advisors are usually compensated in the form of equity points in your business equal to 0.5 - 2% ownership, vested over time, and sometimes with a cash stipend. You must clearly define their time commitment as a certain number of phone calls or meetings each quarter in your Advisory Board Agreement (templates are available online). As shareholders, your advisors become dedicated advocates committed to your success.

Choosing the right advisors depends on where you, or your team, might lack expertise and experience. If you are a medical doctor, then you probably don't need another medical doctor as an advisor, instead you may want a business advisor. For me, most of my endeavors require a certain amount of academic or scientific rigor, so I usually have at least one academic PhD on my advisory board. An advisory board can also serve as a recruiting tool for officers at a later business stage, but I would caution not to use your advisory board as a recruiting tool for investors, unless you specifically want their expertise in raising capital and for M&A, and not their money. It would be akin to asking your therapist on a date. This is different from the old adage of *"if you want money, then ask for advice, but if you want advice, then ask for money"* which is more of a psychological sales tactic for raising money than it is a rule for creating an effective advisory board.

Professional Services: Attorneys, accountants and bankers are another great source for advice, although they are likely the most expensive and, therefore, have some conflict of interest in that regard. Bankers less so, since they don't bill by the hour. They can all give plenty of advice, but won't necessarily help you make decisions, since they don't want any liability. This can often lead to conversations replete with disclaimers, caveats, and creative use of synonyms. However, these should be the most transparent and honest conversations among your counsel. Just like you shouldn't lie to your doctor, you also shouldn't lie to your professional counselors. As an attorney friend of mine tells his clients about how to engage with him: talk early and talk often.

Directors and Officers: Since I mostly covered how to choose these roles in the chapter about *Dance Partners*, I will just add that these people are ironically both your first line of defense in decision making and the most likely to invoke your hubris and posturing, because they are in fact your peers. Knowing how to talk to them without making yourself vulnerable to their criticism is a delicate balance. Just be confident, in both your role and in theirs -- they are there to help you. One bit of advice that I've heeded over the years when working with various Boards is to always make sure that you have something for them to do, whether that be a task, introduction request, or research. Otherwise, they are prone to look for other ways to help you, and that often means they will try to manage you more.

NEGOTIATING

BATNA is a business term that stands for Best Alternative To a Negotiated Agreement (coined by Roger Fisher and William Ury from their book, 'Getting to Yes: Negotiating Without Giving In'). For example, if you are negotiating a sale, you need to understand your best alternatives if the sale doesn't meet your requirements. Not just as a fall-back to walk away from a bad deal, but to better understand and reinforce the value of what you bring to the table. Your BATNA can mean the difference in confidence or vulnerability for *not* having to sell versus *having* to sell.

You should also understand your role as BATNA-man or BATNA-girl. Just as the words "I'm Batman" are followed by bad-guy-ass-whooping, you should always think about BATNA as the masked defender of your business when approaching any external deal; whether that's with customers, vendors, investors, or acquirers. Anyone in your company can be empowered as BATNA-man or BATNA-girl, but this should certainly be the alter-ego of the CEO.

CEO's must always understand the best alternatives for the sake of the business and shareholders, whether you have to seek them out, create them, or wait long enough for them to arrive. When a negotiation seems lost, it will be BATNA-MAN that comes to the rescue. If you have no BATNA, then 'jokers' and 'two-faces' will wreak havoc on your business.

In the fable of the Frog and the Scorpion, the frog makes the mistake of engaging the scorpion in a negotiation that ultimately leaves the frog vulnerable and hapless. In short, the frog trusts the scorpion not to sting him while transporting the scorpion on its back across some water, as a favor. Then the scorpion stings the frog causing them both to drown. Understanding how and when to negotiate with certain people is a real skill that is mostly intuitive at first. If you're not properly prepared, you and your company may become vulnerable. CEOs especially need to be careful when talking to anyone since their words are often interpreted with much more gravity and can turn a polite conversation into a perceived contractual obligation. This pressure can result in a CEO that appears to others as being inaccessible and closed off, when in fact they are simply unable to speak freely, resulting in the 'lonely CEO' phenomenon.

My 4th grade teacher once told my mother, "If Graham could, he would stand by my desk all day and tell me everything he knows." I have indeed found that keeping things to oneself is perhaps the most difficult discipline to master. Some public relations coaching can be helpful, but you can also lean on your co-founders and managers to run interference for you. "Hey Scorpion, cool story bro... let me introduce you to my co-founder the Alligator who can help us qualify this opportunity."

Whether you are making critical decisions or engaged in a heated negotiation, you should feel confident in your training and the trusted partners and counselors that you've selected to support you.

CHAPTER ELEVEN

Bankruptcy

(See what I did there?)

Some of you will stop before you start because you worry too much about failure, like a dancer afraid of falling. Experienced dancers eventually learn to turn a fall into a flourish and keep going -- they don't just walk off the dance floor, they learn and adjust. For the entrepreneur, failure is part of the learning experience, not the end of it.

No one welcomes bankruptcy, or insolvency, but if you don't feel the sting of these at some point, you may not learn how best to avoid them in the future. Although, when my oldest son was 8 years old, he took an interest in mechatronic design and started working with electricity and built his own vending machines. My cousin who has experience in electrical engineering recommended that we find him a "good shop teacher, preferably one missing a finger or two." To his point, you can also learn from others who have experienced the sting of failure before you.

We seem to have a love/hate relationship with failure in our culture. In recent years, the mantra of "fail fast" or "fail forward" has sent many startups to their early demise with the pomp and circumstance of so many Mayan sacrifices; except, instead of feathery headdresses and make-up, we see self-effacing blog posts and books from CEOs and fund managers, but not so much from the Limited Partners (LPs) who actually backed the funds that lost the money! On the flip side of that coin, we mock failure in those we don't like -- former President Donald Trump filed for 6 bankruptcies between 1991-2009 according to Wikipedia, a favorite topic among more liberal news media. In that sense, the negative association with failure seems to be in the eye of the beholder. So, it's no surprise that even the possibility of failure paralyzes so many to move forward.

Failure is also fractal, and relative. There can always be more failure - like a protagonist in a film who is down on their luck and lamenting how 'it couldn't possibly get any worse,' just as it starts to rain. There are degrees of failure, from the benign mistake to the cataclysmic, such as, a business person jumping from a window on the thirteenth floor of a high rise. To that point, here are various perspectives of failure to illustrate the relative nature of this beast and to convey the pain of losing your fingers without having to lose *your* fingers:

The Lifestyle Business - This is a startup that supports its founders and employees with just enough revenue to be at "break even" or be slightly profitable, but not enough revenue to be attractive enough for a liquidation event like an Initial Public Offering (IPO) on the stock market or an M&A event. This is only considered a failure by the company's investors, who may start to ask for their money back, which may or may not trigger the company's demise, depending on how much capital was raised to get to this point and how agreeable the pay back terms. Lifestyle businesses frustrate VCs and investors because even if they get all of their money back with interest, their money is tied up over time that could perhaps have been spent to make even more profit elsewhere. So, when you are raising money and a VC says they think your business is a "lifestyle business," that is what they mean.

The Acqui-Hire - This is when your business is attractive enough to get purchased by another business who will hire a new team, but not necessarily pay your investors back 100%. This provides a safe landing for the founders, but they lose control of their business, and provides a successful M&A metric for its investors even if they don't get 100% of their money back. While it isn't the best outcome, it's considered intrinsically validating to the founders and investors, since they proved the thesis that the business would have a monetary value to a buyer, even if it's not that large for a liquidation event. It's also good for the founders because, after their earn-out period (the period of time they are employed by the new owners to ensure a smooth transition), they can more easily raise funding again as an experienced founder with a "successful exit" under their belt. The VC fund will likewise still label that company as "Acquired!" in their roster of portfolio companies to show their LPs that they are choosing desirable startups.

The Fold - There is a period of time when your startup has raised some angel capital, but not gone into debt with creditors, and maybe hasn't spent all the money it raised. If there is seemingly no path to 10x growth, even if there is potential to be a successful lifestyle business, investors will push hard to make you fold the business and pay them back. This is usually what investors mean when they say you should "fail fast" -- they want to get their money back as soon as possible to reinvest it elsewhere. And maybe they will invest in your next idea. Maybe.

The Zombie Startup - When a startup business hovers above insolvency, either through additional fundraising, debt, or revenue, and barely keeps the lights on, they become what is often referred to as a Zombie Startup. They may be able to keep inflating their valuation with subsequent rounds of funding to keep investors from pulling the plug, since it would also likely trigger a bankruptcy. Zombie startups rarely survive without some kind of restructuring or recapitalization, which usually means their original investors will lose money and the founders will lose control. They are particularly vulnerable to the Strangle Acquisition.

The Strangle Acquisition - This is a more aggressive Acqui-Hire strategy where the acquirer starts with friendly negotiations, but instead waits for the startup to lose more value over time, by either dragging out the M&A discussions until the startup runs out of money, or by slowly hiring away key team members until the company can no longer function and is willing to sell its other assets to the buyer at a reduced price. Sometimes the purchasing company will offer shareholders stock in the new company as compensation, but that's only viable if those stocks are publicly traded and able to be liquidated. If the stocks are still held privately, it's possible that the end result could be that the original startup becomes a shell company operating under a trustee attorney on behalf of its shareholders until the purchasing company's stocks are liquid and able to be sold. This assumes there are some funds to compensate said trustee for an indefinite amount of time, which is unlikely, but I've seen it proposed.

Prepackaged & Restructuring Bankruptcies - This is when a startup business has more debt with creditors than it can pay in a liquidation event, thereby leaving nothing to its investors, and is only able to recapitalize or salvage value for its shareholders through a Chapter 11 bankruptcy and effectively have their assets purchased by other investors, hopefully in a premeditated way, that gives the buyer an advantage of timing in the bankruptcy court. This is mostly a shell game enabled by bankruptcy laws exploited by large corporations. It is what former President Donald Trump is likely referring to in a 2011 interview with Newsweek when he said, "I do play with the bankruptcy laws—they're very good for me." Pre-packaged (aka Pre-Pack) bankruptcies are risky because other eagle-eyed buyers could still bid against the intended buyers and run up the price as in an auction, and a bankruptcy court judge can still rule against the intended deal. This is where collusion with friends in high places can benefit a dishonest entrepreneur, if they can survive the stress.

The Liquidation Bankruptcy - No one really wins in a traditional Chapter 7 bankruptcy. Creditors probably lose money, preferred shareholders (investors) most definitely lose money, and founders lose everything. If you don't have a pre-pack deal, you are at the mercy of the bankruptcy court and judge, who can decide who gets paid back from the liquidation of assets, if any. Usually your creditors will get paid back pennies on the dollar for your debts owed to them, and then shareholders get nothing. For all intents and purposes, this is the ultimate failure for an entrepreneur. But just as there are fates worse than death, there are certainly fates worse than bankruptcy. You can use your imagination.

A dancer never forgets an injury, whether physical like a sprained ankle from a bad landing, or emotional from that time when a person left them on the dance floor. But, the humiliation and feelings of inadequacy move some to better themselves, returning to the dance floor to work on skills, while others might give up and say dancing is not for them. An entrepreneur who has experienced any of the above failures and then returns to build another company is more likely to not make the same mistakes twice.

CHAPTER TWELVE

Success

The world is full of patterns, and once you've been dancing long enough you will see them everywhere you go. Pattern recognition is one of our best tricks, and arguably what makes us human. Once you've experienced one of the many various life cycles of a business, you can recognize milestones of that life cycle in other businesses, and see how opportunity and risk will likely play out. This will help you increase your chances of success both as an entrepreneur and as an investor.

Hard work with all of its ups and downs that we like to call experience, brings with it recognition of holes and traps to avoid, social skills to improve upon, and forks in the roads that force choices both safe and risky. The growing pains of business, as well as the pitfalls and injuries of learning dance, serve to transform a landscape once strange and scary to one that will provide many roads to success. Whether it is finding a great investor, or suddenly having an innate knowledge of where the music is taking you, finding the patterns is so much better than trying to blindly predict the future.

While both success and failure can be in the eye of the beholder, there is no doubt when a business is growing and profitable. The outcomes of that financial success can be lifelong ownership thereby creating generational wealth, selling to either financial or strategic buyers, or going public. Interestingly, these financial boosts don't always guarantee emotional success or happiness, but generally speaking if you took a business from zero to succession, acquisition or IPO, then you will be lauded as a successful entrepreneur and find yourself invited to speak on panel discussions, honored at events, and able to go on to more easily raise funding for your next venture.

Success can also be fickle and ephemeral. When I worked in the Los Angeles entertainment industry, there was a common expression about success, that 'you are only as successful as your next project,' which may have either inspired or been inspired by a quote from the Lakers coach Phil Jackson at that time, "You're only a success for the moment that you complete a successful act." The point being that you can't rest on your laurels. As an entrepreneur you will need to understand this to motivate yourself to keep moving, keep innovating, keep building.

Notice how much shorter this chapter is compared to the previous chapter about failure? That's because we don't learn as much from success as we do failure. Success is sometimes the result of all of your previous lessons, and sometimes the result of dumb luck, but it's not a lesson in and of itself. Either way, it should be celebrated, however short and sweet it may be.

Lasting success would be measured by personal growth and things like your own happiness, your impact on others, or your network. These may get dismissed as subjective, but if you aren't happy and making others happy around you, then you aren't having fun and you probably aren't growing your network in a meaningful way. Afterall, *your network is your net worth*. Your *business* can be a success or a failure, but whether or not *you* are a success or failure has more to do with how you behave, how you help others, and how others in turn want to help you.

CONCLUSION

You may have heard the platitude, 'dance like nobody's watching.' that is often mis-attributed to either Mark Twain, William Purkey, Satchel Paige, Buddha or many others. While its thesis may seem like folksy ancient wisdom, according to the Yale Book of Quotations, it actually originated in 1987 from songwriters Susanna Clark and Richard Leigh in a country song called 'Come From the Heart' popularized by Kathy Mattea.

You've got to sing like you don't need the money

Love like you'll never get hurt

You've got to dance like nobody's watchin'

It's gotta come from the heart if you want it to work.

Each of those lines can be great mantras for the entrepreneur, but we all know what it feels like to dance like nobody's watching... it's exhilarating, maybe a little goofy, and most importantly it's without fear of failure. Even professional dancers on stage in front of judges and patrons will describe their best moments as feeling like the rest of the world had suddenly disappeared and it was just them and the music alone on that stage. Finding that 'zone' in entrepreneurship is no different. Entrepreneurs with their heads down in their work are often disconnected from current events and the trappings of trends in pop culture because nothing else matters to them besides their business and its marketplace.

Although one has to work at learning how to dance, it never feels like work. This should be the same for the entrepreneur. The entrepreneur should never feel like the busiest or hardest working person they know, even if they are. This quality is one that immediately identifies a truly great entrepreneur. They are a servant-leader who is always happy to step in wherever and whenever their team needs help.

Joy in being a pioneer lives inside you and will not totally abandon you, even in the darkest moments. Sometimes, exhausted by self doubt, the doubt of others, difficult investors, and people who want to steal what you have developed, an entrepreneur might want to just sit down and take a break. You mustn't feel regret when this happens because there will almost certainly be a new opportunity around the corner, or you can simply pick up where you left off.

For a dancer, not dancing can be accompanied by a horrible feeling of vacancy that leaves them tired and nervous. It is only when that dancer returns to the dance floor, that their inner system is restored. Likewise, an entrepreneur can feel like they are wandering aimlessly, or like a *has-been* when left stagnant. It is a must for them to return to doing what they love, building businesses and running things.

The world hums along, interrupted by many problems needing solutions. For this reason, entrepreneurs will never become obsolete. As long as there is rhythm, there is opportunity for entrepreneurs to dance.

ACKNOWLEDGEMENTS

This book wouldn't be possible without the help and support of my entire family. For my mother, Elise Boyce, who not only edited this book, but also helped with the dance metaphors – simultaneously leveraging her experience as a professional writer and as a Latin dancer. For my wife, Heather Dodge, and our kids: Luke, Flint, Rex, Dulcie and Zane, who followed me back and forth across the country and held on through the various twists and turns of my career. And for those unique family members willing and able to jump onto my cap table when called upon: Lee Boyce and Frank Russo.

Thanks to all my fellow entrepreneurs, co-founders and co-conspirators, past and present, especially: James Sajor, Mike Belt, Kim Samuelson, Gabby Rose, Dr. Ramesh Raskar, Vitor Pamplona, Bethany LoMonaco, Alison Hjembo, Clayton Graul, Dan Reagan, Stetson Lewis, Tim Chase, Chris and Tracy McCormick, and everyone else at MAGIC, PathCheck Foundation and Johns Hopkins Technology Ventures.

Finally, thanks to all the investors and mentors who have helped me along the way, including Rob Neivert, Elizabeth Yin, Deb Tillett, Paul Palmieri, and especially Brad Feld and David Cohen who have been my coaches from day one at Techstars up to the writing of this book and taught me to always #GiveFirst.

ABOUT THE AUTHOR

Graham Dodge is an award-winning entrepreneur and patented inventor with experience designing and deploying large consumer health platforms and systems of intelligence. He is the co-founder of 6 startups and a mentor to countless others through his work at MAGIC, 1 Million Cups Westminster, Johns Hopkins Technology Ventures, NSF I-Corps and MedHacks. Graham has been honored as a Social Innovation Rockstar by BOLD, featured among Broadband for America's Faces of Innovation and recognized for building one of Entrepreneur Magazine's 100 Brilliant Companies. He is also a technology accelerator veteran as an alumni of Techstars, 500 Startups, and Plug And Play Tech Center.

Graham lives in Westminster, Maryland with his wife and their five kids where he runs two 501(c)3 nonprofit organizations. He is also an Adirondack 46er having climbed all 46 of NY State's Adirondack high peaks.

---

[1] Economic Innovation Group - "Weekly Update on COVID-19's Impact on Business Formation and Entrepreneurship" - Dec 17, 2020 - Jimmy O'Donnell

[2] CB Information Services, Inc. - "The Top 20 Reasons Startups Fail", November 6, 2019

[3] Jan Freeman, Bootstraps and Baron Munchausen, Boston.com, January 27, 2009

[4] Mirjam Tuk, Inhibitory Spillover: Increased Urination Urgency Facilitates Impulse Control in Unrelated Domains, April 5, 2011